...th thanks for support from

C000265102

For more information on exploring
the area contact:
Bridgnorth Visitor Information
Centre (01746)763257
Church Stretton Visitor Information
Centre (01694) 723133
Craven Arms Visitor Information
Centre (01588) 676010
Ironbridge Visitor Information
Centre (01952) 884391
Ludlow Visitor Information Centre
(01584) 875053
Much Wenlock Visitor Infomation
Centre (01952) 727679

Ludlow and the Shropshire Hills, Ironbridge and the Severn Gorge

A Little Souvenir by Philip Ruler

Chris Andrews Publications Ltd

Ludlow

Introduction

Shropshire is a green and pleasant county with a wealth of timber-framed buildings, grand sandstone churches, ruined abbeys and splendid castles and country houses. Yet surprisingly this still largely rural county can justly claim to be the birthplace of the Industrial Revolution. The Ironbridge Gorge, a World Heritage Site since 1986, was where the local mineral wealth was enthusiastically exploited. A key date is 1709 when Abraham Darby first used coke as a fuel for smelting iron. The area is now dotted with museums and monuments which reflect its relatively short-lived industrial past, the most famous being the elegant iron bridge itself.

Shropshire has several other very different but important historic sites: Wroxeter [Viroconium] was the fourth-largest city in Roman Britain and the picturesque town of Much Wenlock was where the Olympic ideal was revived in 1850 by William Penny Brookes .The longest monument in Britain, the eighth century Offa's Dyke, and numerous castles – the finest at Ludlow - are a reminder of the centuries of conflict in this area between the English and Welsh.

All Saints,
Claverley 5

6   The Stable Court at Dudmaston Hall

Shropshire has varied neighbours: it is bordered by 4 English and 2 Welsh counties, from Cheshire in the north to Herefordshire in the south.Its greatest river is the Severn [Sabrina to the Romans], which separates the northern and southern parts of the county. Rising in Wales, it enters the county in the west, flows eastwards to Shrewsbury where it loops round upon itself, then still flowing eastwards it makes the southern boundary of the expanding town of Telford. At Ironbridge it is crossed by the world's first cast-iron bridge. It then flows southwards through Bridgnorth and into Worcestershire. (This book deals with the part of Shropshire situated to the south of the Severn but includes Wroxeter which lies just to its north).

The pre-eminent towns in the southern part of the county are enhanced by their rivers: Bridgnorth by the Severn and Ludlow by the Teme. This river flows below Whitcliffe, a common which provides the visitor with one of the noblest views in lowland England: the town dominated by the medieval castle and church with the Clee Hills as a magnificent backdrop.

Shropshire has impressive hills, they dominate the area and were given official recognition in 1958 when nearly a quarter of the county was designated as the Shropshire Hills Area of Outstanding Natural Beauty. Some of the most spectacular

8   Countryside between Mose and Claverley

of these hills cluster around the little town of Church Stretton: Caer Caradoc and the Lawley are to the north; Wenlock Edge lies to the east and the Long Mynd [the long mountain] to the west. The Clee Hills in the south-east, the Clun forest to the west, the Stiperstones which lie parallel to the Long Mynd and the isolated Wrekin are a further justification for this area's nickname: 'Little Switzerland' and are part of the AONB protected landscape

Shropshire has its place in literature and music. It was the Shropshire Hills that inspired the Worcestershire-born A.E. Housman to write his cycle of poems "A Shropshire Lad". This in turn inspired Vaughan Williams to compose "On

12   Stokesay Castle seen from Nortoncamp Wood

Wenlock Edge", a setting of six of Housman's poems while Ivor Gurney, a Gloucestershire man, also set seven of the poems under the title "Ludlow and Teme". The county also features in the novels of Mary Webb, of which the best-known is "Precious Bane," and in the "Blandings Castle" stories of P.G. Wodehouse.

In Ludlow Shropshire has one of the finest small towns in Great Britain. Despite its small population (just over 10,000 inhabitants) it has nearly 500 listed buildings. Its importance as a cultural and gastronomic centre is remarkable: the food festival based on the castle complements a range of specialist food shops and outstanding restaurants, while the summer festival includes open air performances of Shakespeare in the castle grounds.

With its varied landscape and wealth of wildlife, historic buildings and eventful past, the Shropshire Hills and Severn Gorge is a fascinating area to explore.

The heraldic display of the Earls of Powis dates from 1781

14   Ludlow Castle seen from Whitcliffe

The centre of Ludlow is a harmonious blend of timber framing and mellow Georgian brick   15

16   Ludlow: Dinham Bridge (1823)

Ludlow Church and Castle from the banks of the Teme   17

18 Ludlow has some splendid carvings: seen here in the choir of St Laurence Church and on the Feathers Hotel

Ludlow Castle: the curtain wall of the inner bailey   19

20   Stokesay castle

Stokesay: St John the Baptist and the Gatehouse

22   Stokesay

The gatehouse
seen from the
Hall
23

The Long Mynd

26   Craven Arms came into being as a railway junction. It still receives visits from steam trains as well as modern diesels

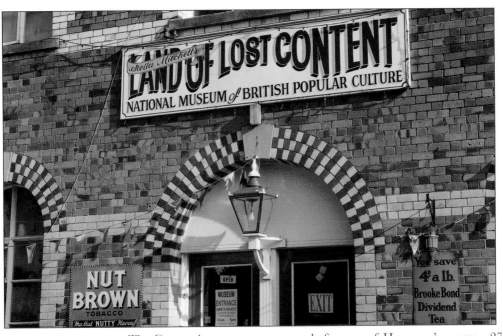

The Craven Arms museum, named after one of Housman's poems 27

28   Clun from the castle: "*The country for easy livers/The quietest under the sun.*"
      - Housman "*A Shropshire Lad*"

The medieval bridge at Clun 29

30   The Stiperstones from Shelve

The quartzite ridge of the Stiperstones 31

32 Wenlock Priory

Holy Trinity and the Guildhall at Much Wenlock   33

34   Arches and archers at Much Wenlock

The Much Wenlock Olympian Games, founded in 1850 by Dr William Penny Brookes are held annually in July

36   Much Wenlock owes its existence to the Cluniac priory whose majestic ruins attract many
visitors

Buildwas Abbey, a Cistercian foundation lies a few miles to the north of Wenlock Priory   37

38 Wroxeter Roman Town

On Wenlock Edge looking westwards

42   Ironbridge with St Luke's Church

The first cast iron bridge in the world, erected in 1779, is the centrepiece of the Ironbridge Gorge World Heritage site

44 The bridge was designed by Thomas Pritchard and cast by Abraham Darby III. It has a span of 31 metres with an arch rising 15.5 metres above normal water level

46 Jackfield Bridge, half a mile downstream from its more famous cousin

The approach to the older bridge is well guarded

Ironbridge 'B' Power Station 47

48   High Town and the church of St Leonard in Bridgnorth

50   Castle Gardens, Bridgnorth

The almost verticle railway links High Town and Low Town   51

52   The old Vicarage at Claverley, spring and autumn

Claverley Churchyard 53

54 All Saints, Claverley: the nave paintings date from c 1200

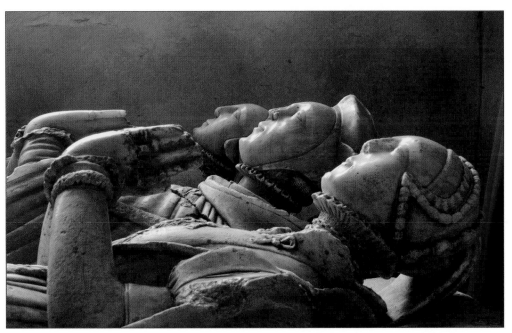

Claverley: the tomb of Sir Robert Broke and his two wives 55

Cleobury Mortimer

58   Cleobury Mortimer

Titterstone Clee Hill from the west   59

60 The Severn Valley Railway at Hampton Loade

62   Ludlow Food festival in the castle grounds

Bishops Castle rooftops   63

Burford House

First published 2010 by Chris Andrews Publications Ltd, 15 Curtis Yard, North Hinksey Lane, Oxford. OX2 0LX

Telephone: +44(0)1865 723404 **www.cap-ox.com** © Chris Andrews Publications Ltd

ISBN 978–1–906725–19–8

Photos and text by Philip Ruler. With thanks to Andrea and Jeffrey Hammersley, Bruce Davies. Also Jo Bickerton at Shropshire Council and Stephanie Hayes at The Shropshire Hills AONB

Front Cover: Ludlow   Back cover: Near Mose

Ludlow and The Shropshire Hills, Ironbridge and The Severn Gorge

Also available in this series:

Herefordshire
Worcestershire
Stratford upon Avon
The Cotswolds South
The Cotswolds North
Bath
Cheltenham
Oxford
Gargoyles and grotesques
Henley on Thames
Winchester
London
Windsor and Eton
The Thames
The Peak District

Guernsey
Sark
Herm
Alderney
Jersey
Undersea Guernsey
Undersea Jersey
Wildfowers of The Channel Islands

Chris Andrews Publications Ltd

Chris Andrews work is known throughout England and the Channel Islands, and is seen in a variety of publications including calendars, posters, fine art prints and books. For information on all our publications please see
www.cap-ox.co.uk
Tel 01865 723404

The Shropshire Hills Area of Outstanding Natural Beauty

There are 49 AONBs in the U.K. and together with National Parks they make up our finest landscapes. The Shropshire Hills Discovery Centre in Craven Arms is an excellent introduction to the area and explains how and who has shaped this beautiful landscape